Average Joe Cyclist Guide:
How to Buy Used Bikes on Craigslist, Kijiji, eBay, LesPAC and Other Online Market Places

If you find this guide useful, you might also like:
**Average Joe Cyclist Guide:
How to Buy the Right Electric Bike**
(available on Kindle and Amazon)
and my cycling blog, **www.averagejoecyclist.com**,
which has tons of free information

Published by Brave New World Publishing

Copyright © 2012 Average Joe Cyclist
All rights reserved
www.averagejoecyclist.com

All rights reserved. No part of this publication may be reproduced, stored in a retrieval system, or transmitted, in any form or by any means, without the prior written permission of the copyright owner.

Disclaimer: The author and the publisher specifically disclaim any responsibility for any liability, loss or risk, personal or otherwise, which is incurred as a consequence, directly or indirectly, of the use and application of any of the contents of this book.

**Average Joe Cyclist Guide:
How to Buy Used Bikes on Craigslist, Kijiji, eBay, LesPAC and Other Online Market Places**

Table of Contents

A Bargain or a Rip-off – Which will it Be?.................. 1
Possible Extra Costs to Consider 2
Know your Bike Terminology 4
    Kinds of Shimano Components, from
        Highest to Lowest Quality............................. 15
Road, Hybrid or Mountain Bike?................................ 20
    Road Bikes 20
    Hybrid Bikes 20
    Mountain Bikes 21
    Cruisers 21
    Touring (Trekking) Bikes 21
Know your Bike Size 22
    Adult Hybrid and Mountain Bike Sizes 23
    Adult Road Bike Sizes 23
    Height and Inseam 24
    Kid's Bike Sizes... 24
Should you Budget for a Bike Fitting?........................ 25
Research Reviews of the Bike on the Internet......... 26
    Verify the Year of Manufacture 27
Research New Bike Prices 28

Research Used Bike Prices 30
Check the Condition of the Bike before
    you Buy 32
Ride before you Buy 36
Red Flags to Watch out For 37
Phrases to Watch out For, and What they
    REALLY Mean 40
Moronic Sellers to Watch out For! 42
General Guidance from Bike Experts 47
Good Quality Bikes made in the Last Couple
    of Decades 50
Good Quality Vintage Bikes 54
Bikes to Strenuously Avoid 55
Making Lemonade … Dedicated Cyclists who
    Fix "Less Worthy" Bikes 56
Should You Buy a "Sucky" Bike? 58
Bargains Can be Found! 59
Tips for Selling Bikes Online 61
A Closing Thought – Please be Nice to
    Bike Sellers 63

Preface

This guide to buying bikes online is a labor of love that grew from a blog post. Last year I did a blog post about the pleasures and perils of buying bikes online, and it turned out to be my most popular post ever. Not only that, but I was deluged with emails from readers, asking me questions about aspects that I had not covered in my post. I realized there is a huge need for guidance on how to find bargain-priced bikes online – and also on how to avoid being ripped off. I was spending so much time answering questions, I decided I might just as well put it all into a book that everyone could access!

This book includes a guide to terminology used in ads; explains how to determine your bike size; shows how to assess the quality of bike components; warns about extra costs, and about poor-quality bikes to avoid; explains how to research new and used bike prices; provides a list of recommended high-quality bikes; explains how to check a bike's condition; provides tips for spotting bike thieves; suggests how to evaluate the asking price of a bike; explains how to verify the age of a bike; and warns about red flags to watch out for.

This guide answers all the questions I have been asked, and then some. I have tried my hardest to give you, the reader, as much value for money as possible, and have included everything I could possibly think of to help you with your bargain hunting. If I've left out something, please feel free to contact me via my blog, ***www.averagejoecyclist.com***, and I will do my best to include it in the next edition of this guide.

Online market places provide a great place to find bargains, providing you know what you are doing. This book will make sure that you do.
Happy bike shopping!

A Bargain or a Rip-off – Which will it Be?

Buying a used bike is one of the cheapest ways in the world to get fit, lose weight, save money and have fun. For between $100 and $250 you can find a decent bike that should not require much fixing; and for $250 to $500 you could find a really great bike that would cost you well upwards of $1,000 new.

However, buying used bikes on Craigslist, Kijiji or any other online source is most certainly a case of **Caveat Emptor – Buyer Beware!** This buyer's guide will help you to buy a good bike online at a good (and sometimes great!) price, and will also help you to avoid getting ripped off. This guide is intended for the average person who doesn't know a whole lot about bikes, and just wants to learn enough to avoid being ripped off – and hopefully to be able to spot the bargains when they come up.

There are bargains to be had, without a doubt. Lots of people have great bikes that they just don't use, which you may be able to buy at a bargain price. But there are also potentially serious pitfalls, to which I will alert you.

Possible Extra Costs to Consider

Bear in mind that the price you pay for the bike will almost certainly not be the full price. This is because it is essential to take a used bike to a bike shop and have it checked, after you have bought it. If you don't get a used bike checked (and probably serviced), you run the risk of a potentially serious accident. So it really is best to pay to have your newly acquired bike properly checked. If it needs to be serviced you will of course have to pay for that, and you may also have to pay to replace a part or two. You may have to get the saddle and handlebar height adjusted, if you don't know how to do it yourself.

If you plan to commute on the bike, you may have to add mud flaps, a kickstand, a good set of lights, a bell and a **rear-view mirror**. The last-mentioned is an excellent safety feature that I highly recommend. Mine has saved my life more than once. If there's something dangerous behind you, it's best to know about it. Generally rear-view mirrors are not considered cool, but I gave up on cool long ago. Besides, as I often tell my kids, I would rather be an uncool live person than a really cool corpse.

Another really excellent investment if you plan to commute to work regularly is a set of **puncture-resistant tires**. For a few extra dollars, you can save yourself many hours of unnecessary frustration and hassle: flat tires can make you late for work, cause you major inconvenience, and just generally ruin your day. And believe me, if you're going to commute in a big city, your tires are most definitely going to ride over many different things that could give you a sudden puncture.

So in short, you could be looking at anywhere from $30 to a couple of hundred dollars to get your new-but-used bike ready to roll.

The best advice is to try and buy a bike that matches your needs as closely as possible, and that is in really good shape.

For example, many people sell perfectly good, **fully-fitted commuter bikes** online. If commuting by bike is your goal, this can be an excellent bargain. Buying all those bits and pieces adds up to a whole heap of money very quickly (as I know from long and bitter experience).

One more word on costs – **try not to push up your costs by buying out of your area** and having to pay shipping costs. Not only is this costly, but it exposes you to the risk of being scammed.

It's best to buy local!

Know your Bike Terminology

This list is intended for those fairly new to cycling, to help decipher terms that show up in adverts for bikes. Knowing the meaning of these terms will help you decide if you want to look at a particular bike. Some of these terms are included because they are mentioned in **"Check the Condition of the Bike"** on p. 32.

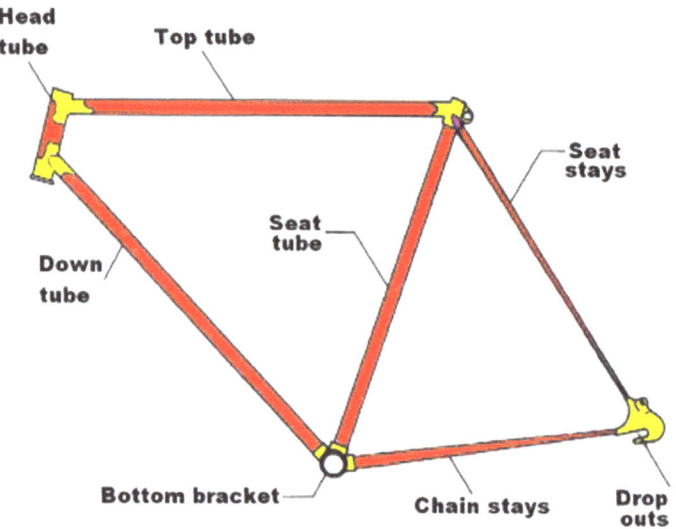

- **Aluminum bikes** – these have frames made of aluminum, which have become the default for most modern bikes. They tend to be lighter than steel bikes, and have fatter tubes.
- **ATBs** – all-terrain bikes – see Mountain bikes on p. 11.
- **BMX bikes** – bicycle motocross bikes, also called stunt bikes, used for tricks. Smaller bikes, with bare bones accessories, but often fitted with special equipment, such as pegs to stand on.
- **Bottom bracket** – the part to which the cranks attach.
- **Caliper brakes** – see **Rim brakes**, below.

- ☐ **Cantilever brakes** – see **Rim brakes**, below.
- ☐ **Carbon-fibre bikes** – these have frames made of carbon-fibre and are very light, but very expensive. They are not as strong as aluminum or steel. Some aluminum bikes do incorporate carbon parts. For example, carbon forks are fairly common on higher-end hybrids and road bikes, and are good at taking some of the edge off bumpy urban roads.
- ☐ **Components** – Refers to the pieces that are added to the frame to equip the bike, such as the gear system, brakes, shift levers, crank set and pedals, seatpost, handlebars and derailleurs. Better quality bikes have better quality components. An ad that says something like "top of the line components" indicates that the bike has better quality components. Of course, to be absolutely sure the seller is telling the truth you would have to research the components (see **Kinds of Shimano Components** on p. 15).
- ☐ **Cranks** – the part to which the pedals attach.
- ☐ **Chromoly** – Chrome Molybdenum Steel. A light, strong steel, often used to build fairly light, responsive, long-lasting frames. Sometimes called CRO MO.
- ☐ **Cruiser bikes or cruisers** – these usually have balloon tires, upright seating posture, and

How to Buy Used Bikes Online

single-speed drivetrains. They are pretty simple steel bikes, often incorporating quite stylish and fun designs. They are heavy but strong. They were very popular from the 1930s to the 1950s, and in recent times have become popular again. These are great bikes for riding in a leisurely way around a park, and they have many fans. In fact, if you live in a major city you might find a Cruiser Club you can join. However, personally I would not recommend them for commuting, touring or any kind of serious cycling.

- ☐ **Cyclocross bikes –** specialty bikes for cyclo-cross races. Much like road bikes, except the tires are fatter, and there are some other differences as well. If you don't know what they are, you probably don't need one (very few people do).
- ☐ **Derailleurs –** the name derailleurs comes from railway line derailleurs, because these are the things that move the chain from one chain ring onto the next. There are two of them, one at the front of the chain and one at the back. They are a high-maintenance part of the bike, needing frequent cleaning and oiling (like the chain). They are also very important to maintain – clean derailleurs will help keep your bike going well.

- ☐ **Disc brakes** – most commonly fitted to mountain bikes, disc brakes are heavier and more expensive than other kinds of brakes. Due to their weight and the fact that they work best with fat tires, they are almost never seen on road bikes. Basically they consist of a metal disc attached to the wheel hub. When the cyclist pulls on the brakes, pads squeeze the disc, slowing the wheel as kinetic (motion) energy is converted into thermal (heat) energy. There are two kinds of disc brakes: **hydraulic disc brakes** and **mechanical disc brakes.** Hydraulic disc brakes are considered superior and are more expensive than mechanical disk brakes. Personally I love hydraulic disc brakes on my commuter and mountain bikes, as they give you higher precision braking, and are especially useful when commuting in very wet weather. However, rim brakes also do a fine job of stopping your bike. **You do not have to have disc brakes**.
- ☐ **E-bikes** – see **Electric bikes**, below.
- ☐ **Electric bikes** – bikes with electric assists, which make it easier to cycle up hill, and to cycle in general. Most of these offer a combination of pedaling and electrical assist, with the assist

Terminology

powered by a rechargeable battery. These bikes are wonderful as they make cycling more accessible for people who are older or who have physical ailments, such as knee problems. They also make it feasible for physically able people to commute long distances without excessive exhaustion or sweat. In fact, research indicates that people who buy electric bikes get fitter than people who buy regular bikes – simply because if you have an electric bike, you are more likely to use it for daily commuting. These bikes are not covered in this guide, as they are a massive, specialized subject. If you are interested in an electric bike, you might want to check out **Average Joe Cyclist Guide: How to Buy the Right Electric Bike** (available on Kindle and Amazon).

☐ **Fixed gear bikes, also know as Fixies –** bikes that use a rear drive system, do not have a freewheel, and cannot coast. The pedals attach directly to the rear hub. Essentially you have to keep pedaling all the time, as these bikes usually have only a front brake, and sometimes have no brakes at all. When they have no brakes, you stop the bike by pedaling backwards. They usually only have one gear, as well. Why anyone would want one is beyond me, but if you do, please try before you buy, because they require a very different riding style. I remember I had one of these once, when I was a very little boy, and I recall having to brake by stamping down hard on the pedals. I was very happy to graduate to a real bike ... However, these bikes now apparently have "hipster-cool," so you can expect to pay more for them, even though they have less features.

- **Fork** – this is the part that houses the front wheel. It is attached to the main bike frame, and consists of two blades (most round, some flat) that travel downward to hold the front axle, thus allowing the cyclist to steer. Some have suspension built into them, others do not.

- **Frame prices** – the hierarchy of frame prices usually goes like this: low-end steel, low-end aluminum, low-end carbon, high-end aluminum, high-end steel and high-end carbon.

- **Full suspension bikes** – bikes with front and rear suspension, as below (see also **Suspension**).

☐ **Hardtail** – a bike that has front suspension but does not have rear suspension.
☐ **Head tube** – the tube that contains the headset (steering bearings). The top and down tubes attach to this tube (see illustration on p. 4).
☐ **Hybrid bikes** – a cross between road bikes and mountain bikes, and a good choice for commuting in the urban jungle (see picture below). Not-so-young people sometimes find hybrids are easier on their backs. The tires are thinner than mountain bikes, but thicker than road bikes. (Tires can be changed, but only as much as the rims permit – for example, it is impossible to put a fat mountain bike tire on a thin road bike rim.) Hybrids have straight handlebars, and usually have a fairly upright riding position. Upright is good for riding in traffic, as you can see better. Bear in mind that riding position can be adjusted quite cheaply, by changing the handlebars or the riser (the part that attaches the handlebars to the frame).

☐ **Hydraulic disk brakes** – see **Disc brakes** on p. 7.

Average Joe Cyclist Guide

- **Lug or Lugged (frame)** – some ads will proudly refer to a lugged frame. This refers to short angled tubes that are used to join and reinforce two or more tubes on a bicycle frame. They tend to make the bike frame stronger, and can look pretty good too. The vintage Bianchi frame above has lugs that are chromed, making them easier to see.
- **Mechanical disk brakes** – see **Disc brakes** on p. 7.
- **Mixte/Step-through** – these bikes do not have a cross bar, making it easy to step on or off. They are sometimes called "lady's bikes," but in fact they are popular with all gender persuasions. They are especially useful if you have limited mobility, or are nervous because you haven't been on a bike for three or four decades. They are also great if you want to bike in a skirt.
- **Mountain bikes** – (also called all-terrain bikes or ATBs) bikes designed primarily for off road use, with straight handlebars, a strong (but heavier) frame, and fat (but again heavier) tires. Many have suspension shocks on the front, which add comfort (at the expense of weight). A feature I really like is suspension shocks with a lockout –

Terminology

this means you can turn off the shocks when you don't want or need them. Although these bikes are called mountain bikes, many never go off road, as they are also suitable for rough urban commuting. Bear in mind that their weight means you have to pedal harder for the same speed you could more easily achieve on a hybrid or a road bike. That's why, if you take a look at the flocks of urban cycle-commuters that are becoming increasingly common in modern cities, you will see far more road bikes than mountain bikes. The photo above shows what you **could** do with a mountain bike, but if you're not quite this athletic, don't worry – research shows that 95% of people who own mountain bikes **never** ride them on mountains, or even take them off road.

- ☐ **Pedelec –** a bike that also has an electric motor, which helps cyclists to pedal but does not replace pedaling.
- ☐ **Recumbent bikes (recumbents) –** bikes on which the seat is tilted back and low to the ground, usually with the pedals on top of the front wheel. Although it looks as if the rider is lying down, recumbent bikes are in fact said to be the fastest type of bike because they are so aerodynamic. Helpful for people with bad backs, too.

☐ **Rigid bike** – a bike with no suspension. Note this is not a bad thing – many of my favorite bikes are rigid! Suspension adds comfort, but it also adds weight, thereby decreasing cycling efficiency. It's also just another set of parts that can go wrong, and therefore just another set of parts that could be faulty on a used bike.

☐ **Rim brakes** – as the cyclist applies the brakes, friction pads apply braking force to the rims of the wheels, slowing the bike down. Rim brakes are cheap and easy to maintain, but are not great in wet weather (especially on steel rims). On the plus side, you can upgrade these kinds of brakes simply by buying better quality **brake pads**, which do not cost a lot of money. (Even if you buy a brand new bike, this is an area where manufacturers often save money by using low-quality pads, so even with a new bike you might want to upgrade the pads.) There are various kinds of rim brakes, including V-brakes, caliper brakes and cantilever brakes. **Caliper brakes** (below left) are self-contained, and are attached to the bike's frame with a single bolt. The arms reach downward and therefore need to be long enough to get around the tire. **Cantilever brakes** (below right) attach to the side of the frame or fork, requiring special brazed-on fittings on the frame. The brake consists of

two separate arms, each of which is individually attached to the frame or fork. **V-brakes** (see also **V-brakes** on p. 18) developed from cantilever brakes, and are considered the most cost-efficient way to achieve powerful and reliable braking. However, the older style cantilever brakes are well suited to the design of road bikes.

- ☐ **Road bikes (also called racing bikes) –** a lightweight bike with thin tires and (usually) drop handlebars, built for speed and a more aggressive style of cycling (your back is close to parallel to the road when your hands are in the drops).  Although primarily built for racing, many people do use them for commuting. They are certainly the most efficient and fastest bikes.

- ☐ **Shimano –** countless ads will mention that the bike has "Shimano components" or "Shimano gears." This means that the bike's components or gears were made by a Japanese manufacturing company called Shimano. For your purposes, this means close to nothing at all. **Shimano has 50% of the world market in bicycle components,** which means that they supply a full range of products, from bottom of the range to top of the range. A Shimano product could be close to garbage, or close to heaven. To find out which, use the tables supplied below. Or you can just ignore the allusion to Shimano, and examine other aspects of the bike. You can take a little comfort from the thought that as Shimano manufactures components for some of the world's greatest bikes, there must be some kind of positive trickle-down effect to the rest of its product line. (Shimano's primary competition are bicycle component manufacturers Campagnolo and SRAM).

The table below will help you to figure out if a bike is a good buy, as it shows you the **level of quality of various Shimano parts** (top quality is at the top). The top levels are very expensive, and are mainly used on expensive race bikes; **the average cyclist does not need the top levels**. For example, Deore is good enough for the average cyclist's mountain bike – and Deore is only four levels from the bottom. In road bikes, the highest level I have ever owned is 105, and although I found those components **awesome**, I really did not need that level, as I am not even a casual racer. Tiagra and even Sora components are suitable for beginning and casual riders.

Kinds of Shimano Components, from highest to lowest quality

Mountain Bikes	Road, Hybrid, & Touring Bikes
XTR	Dura Ace Electronic
XT	Dura Ace
Deore LX	Ultegra
SLX (starting in 2009)	LX (starting in 2009)
Deore	105
Alivio	Alfine
Acera	Tiagra
Altus	Nexus
	Sora

Note that there is **one more level**, right at the very bottom: Shimano parts with no model numbers or names; these are made for department store bikes, and are cheap and nasty. So just because the ad says "Shimano", this does not mean you are buying quality. **Find out what kind of Shimano parts they are, and compare with the table to see where they fall.**

- **Single speed** – these bikes only have one gear. They are popular at the moment, for reasons that escape me. My daughter wants one, which prompted me to ask her, "Why would you not take advantage of a century of advances in cycling technology?" To which her response was a withering look of pity, and a grunted "They're cool." I still think they're stupid, and they certainly make it hard to get up hills, or even to get the bike started. On the plus side, they're usually cheaper and lighter than geared bikes. And they don't have a geared derailleur system, so that is one less thing that can get dirty or broken – and one less thing that could be faulty on a used bike.
- **Steel bikes** – these have frames made of steel. Steel is a little heavier than some materials, but it

is flexible and makes for a comfortable ride. Most older bikes are made of steel. **There is nothing wrong with a steel bike – don't be taken in by the idea that you have to have an aluminum bike.**

- **Suspension –** a system that suspends a cyclist so that the ride is not so bumpy. (See also **Hardtail** and **Full suspension bikes**, above.) Most common on mountain bikes, but also used on many hybrids. The suspension is most commonly built into the front fork, but may also be built into the rear of the bike, or the seat post or the hub. Mountain bikes with both front and rear suspension are becoming more common, and are referred to as full suspension bikes. Good ones are still very expensive. If you are buying a used full suspension bike, bear in mind that people who own these bikes often ride hard on rough terrain, or fearlessly hurtle down mountainsides, so the bike may have been soundly thrashed and possibly damaged. Check these even more carefully than regular bikes.
- **Touring bikes –** (also called Trekking bikes) bikes designed to handle the demands of cycle

touring. Cycle touring by definition entails cycling long distances while carrying heavy loads, and touring bikes are adapted to facilitate this. For example, they may have a longer wheelbase, so that your heels do not bang into your saddle bags when pedaling (a very annoying thing). They are designed to be especially strong, and the frames have several mounting points so that multiple panniers and luggage holders can be carried. They are usually designed for comfort as well, given that bike tourists may spend many hours of the day in the saddle. (To find out more about bike touring, visit the world's most popular bike touring blog: http://bicycletouringpro.com/blog/ – the source of the great photo on the previous page.)

☐ **Trailer bikes** – a bike that is trailed along by another bike in front. A tow bar hooks it to the bike that is pulling it. The trailer bike just has a back wheel, a seat, pedals and handlebars for the young rider to hold on to. These are designed for younger riders so that they can safely join their parents on rides. The person in front needs to be fit and strong!

☐ **V-brakes** – these were developed by Shimano from cantilever brakes. (See also **Rim brakes**, on p. 13.) V-brakes are a side-pull version of cantilever brakes and, like cantilever brakes, are mounted

on the frame. V-brakes or disc brakes are best for mountain bikes. The photo of V-brakes is from the website http://sheldonbrown.com/home.html — a great resource for the cycling community, generously created by the late, great Sheldon Brown. Check it out if you want to learn much, much more about bikes.

☐ **Vintage –** in popular usage (and especially in advertising!) the word "vintage" means "Characterized by excellence, maturity, and enduring appeal; classic." Many older bikes are advertised as vintage. As with cars and people, **old age does not necessarily equate to excellence** … so this is definitely a case of **Buyer Beware!** If you are attracted to a bike advertised as "vintage," do a lot of research to make sure you are buying finely-aged quality (rather than simply clearing something rusty out of someone else's garage). See also **"Good Quality Vintage Bikes"** on p. 54.

☐ **Women-specific bikes (also called Women Specific Design, or WSD) –** some bike manufacturers now make bikes that they have tried to modify to fit differences in anatomy between men and women. The frame geometry may be slightly different (for example, the top tube is usually shorter), the brake and gear controls will typically be smaller, and the wheels may be smaller. But remember that everyone is different, and not all women need a WSD bike. As with everything else with bikes, the key is to find a bike that feels good to you, personally. So if you're a man, don't run away screaming if the bike has a teeny little "WSD" somewhere on the frame!

Road, Hybrid or Mountain Bike?

This is the **first and most important decision you need to make about your future bike.** The decision will be based on personal preference, and on how you plan to use the bike. For example, if you want to commute, you could choose a road bike or a hybrid. Each type of bike has pros and cons.

Road Bikes

Ideal for fit people who want to cycle far and fast, as they are certainly the most efficient bikes in terms of converting your power to forward propulsion. The first time I had a good quality road bike, I was astonished at how the bike seemed to want to go fast, like a race horse! Because of their efficiency, many people choose these for commuting, but there is a trade-off: you may feel the potholes more, your thinner tires are more vulnerable, and you should not do any curb jumping! Some people don't want a road bike because they don't like drop handlebars, but you can now get road bikes with straight handlebars.

Hybrid Bikes

Hybrids are a great choice for all-round versatility. They're tougher than road bikes, but not as heavy as mountain bikes. A good choice if you want to commute, or if you want to ride the local trails.

Average Joe Cyclist Guide

Mountain Bikes

You could commute on a mountain bike, but it would be slower. But as they are tougher, you would be able to jump on and off curbs! If you want to explore trails on a mountain, you need a mountain bike, and a front suspension mountain bike will probably do you just fine. If however you are fearless and athletic, you might want to consider a full-suspension mountain bike, so that you can hurtle down mountains, leap over logs, grab some "big air" and just generally carry on like a weekend superhero.

Cruisers

These are usually steel bikes, with fatter, small tires. Not as efficient as most other bikes, but they are fun. Great if you want to look cool while cruising down to Starbucks. Ideal if you want to cruise sedately along city cycle paths with friends and family. There are some astonishingly cool cruisers out there. Some of the newer ones combine modern components with creative retro styling.

Touring (Trekking) Bikes

Great if you want to go on vacation on a bike. Tougher than most bikes, with more options for carrying luggage. They may have drop handlebars or straight, and they often have a longer wheelbase so you can carry more luggage (without your heels banging into your panniers).

Know your Bike Size

Bikes have sizes that are based on the height of the bicycle, measuring the length of the seat post tube. **It is really important to know your bike size.** You don't want to waste your time (and the seller's time) by going to view bikes that are too small or too large. One way to find your bike size is to go to a bike shop and try out a couple of bikes. Or, if you don't want to waste the bike shop's time, you can **figure out your bike size with the tables on the next page**. Of the two lengths (height and inseam), inseam is the most important.

Note: to make it a bit more complicated, there are different bike sizing systems. There's one system for road bikes, and then a different one that is used for mountain bikes and hybrid bikes. So **first decide what kind of bike you want, then figure out your size, and you will be good to go!** One little catch is that many (unbelievably many) bike advertisers forget to include the size (see below in the "Moronic Sellers" section), so you have to make that inquiry first.

Personally I have made the mistake of buying a bike that is too big, just because the price was right and I loved the bike. Big mistake! I could never get completely comfortable on the bike, and eventually I had to sell it. I hate to admit that I actually made this mistake twice! (I'm just a sucker for a pretty bike.) It's an expensive, time-wasting mistake, so don't do like I did, do like I say!

Start by knowing your bike size, and then double-check: can you comfortably stand over the cross-bar, without hurting any part of your body? Will you be able to stop safely, or will you have to fall gracelessly sideways until your feet make contact with the earth? If the bike hurts you when you are standing over it, or is too big to stop safely, you will not have fun with the bike. Conversely, if the bike is too small, your knees and back will probably start to hurt, and you won't be able to deploy your body power efficiently (plus you will look funny!).

Adult Hybrid and Mountain Bike Sizes

Your Height	Inseam Length	Bike Frame Size
4'11" to 5'3"	25" to 27"	13" to 15"
5'3" to 5'7"	27" to 29"	15" to 17"
5'7" to 5'11"	29" to 31"	17" to 19"
5'11" to 6'2"	31" to 33"	19" to 21"
6'2" to 6'4"	33" to 35"	21" to 23"
6'4" and up	35"	23"

Adult Road Bike Sizes

Your Height	Inseam Length	Bike Frame Size
4'10" to 5'1"	25.5" to 27"	46 to 48 cm
5'0" to 5'3"	26.5" to 28"	48 to 50 cm
5'6" to 5'9"	29.5" to 31"	52 to 54 cm
5'8" to 5'11"	30.5" to 32"	56 to 58 cm
5'10" to 6'1"	31.5" to 33"	58 to 60 cm
6'0" to 6'3"	32.5" to 34"	60 to 62 cm
6'2" to 6'5"	34.5" to 36"	62 to 64 cm

Bike Size

Height and Inseam

The tables on the previous page show bike sizes based on height and inseam. **Note that for adults, inseam is the most important measurement, because it determines your standover height.**

For example, a bike might be advertised as having a standover height of 27 inches. If your inseam is 29 inches, this means that you could stand up with this bike under you, and the cross bar would not damage your most delicate bits. (Obviously this is less important with step through style bikes that do not have a cross bar.)

For road bikes you need to have about 1 to 3 inches of distance between the bar and your crotch; for mountain bikes you would be safer with a bit more.

Kid's Bike Sizes

Child's Age	Child's Height	Wheel Size
2 to 5	26" to 34"	12"
4 to 8	34" to 42"	16"
6 to 9	42" to 48"	18"
8 to 12	48" to 56"	20"
Youth	56" to 62"	24"

Should you Budget for a Bike Fitting?

Here's **another cost that you might want to factor into your plans to buy a bike**. If you're over 30, and/or have any physical issues with your back or neck, it might not be enough just to buy the right bike size. Consider getting a professional bike fitting after you've bought the bike. This can be expensive, but it's worth every penny.

I am over 30 (by quite a long way) and have had back problems, and I find it essential to have newly-acquired bikes professionally fitted. If I don't, I end up with serious backache after long bike rides. Basically the bike fitter measures everything, gets me to sit and pedal on the bike, and finally writes a "prescription" for my bike shop. The last prescription I got recommended raising the handlebars by two inches, and decreasing the "reach" by another two inches, which the bike shop achieved by putting a new riser on the bike. I spent about $35 at the bike shop, and ended up with a bike that is custom fitted to match my body exactly – and I never get back pain after riding the bike. My wife had given up cycling completely because it kept giving her back spasms, so she tried getting her bike professionally fitted, and since then she has been able to ride without pain. Now she's started commuting to work on her bike!

If you can afford it, **I highly recommend having a professional bike fitting after purchasing a used or new bike**. Find a professional fitter on Google, or by asking at your nearest bike shop or physiotherapist. Often they work out of sports physiotherapy offices.

Research Reviews of the Bike on the Internet

Once you know your size and have an idea what kind of bike you would like, you are ready to start searching the online ads. Whether you use Craigslist, Kijiji, eBay, LesPAC or any other online market place is purely a matter of personal preference – they are all good places to look.

Once you find a bike that sounds interesting, the **best advice I can give you is to spend a few minutes on Google, reading everything you can find about the bike, especially reviews**.

As an example: let's assume you have figured out that based on your needs, what you are looking for is a road bike, size 54 cm, price range between $400 and $900. You search the ads, and you come up with an advert that reads "2009 Specialized Sequoia road bike 54 cm – $850." So you know it's the right size, the right kind and the right price range; now it is time to start doing a bit more research. To do this, go to Google (or whatever Search engine you prefer) and type in the bike name and the word "Reviews," as in "Specialized Sequoia 2009 reviews." This search will

bring up tons of good information. Some of it will be contradictory, as people tend to have different opinions, but overall you will definitely see a trend.

What you will learn from this search is that most owners love this bike, and that it is renowned for being a very comfortable, endurance road bike. That means you could comfortably ride it for very long distances. You will also learn that it is a high-quality road bike, and is referred to as an entry-level racing bike. In other words, you could use it to do your very first road race, or to participate in a social biking event such as the Enbridge Ride to Conquer Cancer. So if this is your plan, you are on the right track, and this bike is a definite possibility.

But even though you know that this is a good bike, **you still don't know whether $850 is a fair asking price. That's why you also need to research new and used bike prices**.

Verify the Year of Manufacture

Most years, bikes are only made in one specific color. This gives you an excellent way to verify sellers' claims. For example, I recently saw a 2011 Specialized Dolce road bike advertised for $749 on Craigslist. A pretty good price – eBay showed me that the same year and model bike had recently been sold for $999. But the catch was that the photo showed a dark red bike. If you Google "2011 Specialized Dolce" (and I did), you will find that **there is no such thing as a red 2011 Specialized Dolce**. That year, all of those bikes were manufactured in white. This shows you that the seller is not to be trusted. My suspicions were verified when the ad changed a few days later, with the photo replaced by a generic photo, and the year of manufacture deleted from the posting. Price stayed the same, though! But as my Google searching had made me pretty sure it was a 2008, and other people were posting the same year and model for around $550, I was not interested.

Research New Bike Prices

Once you know what kind of bike you would like to buy, go online or go to a bike shop, and check the prices of new bikes. That way, you will be more informed about whether you are getting a bargain or not. This is necessary because there are people who post used bikes at outrageously high prices. That might be because they are trying to rip people off. However, it might just be sheer ignorance about the price of the new articles, such as might be the case with someone selling off his kid's bike after the child grows up and leaves home. **Bottom line: it's up to you to know a thing or two about prices**.

For example, I would not pay $350 for a brand-new bike from Sears (actually I might pay almost that much to AVOID riding a Sears bike) – so why would I pay that much for one that is close to 40 years old? But I have seen such absurd offers actually advertised online …

In our example above, the 2009 Sequoia Specialized, you would need to go to the Specialized website and research new bike prices. There you would encounter a common problem in bike price research – Specialized no longer sells bikes called Sequoia. But don't despair, all you have to do is look for a similar kind of bike.

A little research will show you that the Specialized Secteur Sport Triple is also an entry-level road/racing bike, admired by users for its comfort and speed, and with similar components to the Sequoia. But you can get a new one for $1,100. Not only that, but the bike at the bottom of this range, the Specialized Secteur Triple, would probably meet your needs just as well, and this one only costs $880 new! This tells you that the asking price on the Sequoia is too high, and you need to keep looking if you want to find a bargain – or you need to see if the seller will accept a more reasonable offer. **Show him or her your research, and he or she may just be willing to see reason and accept a more realistic price.**

Here's another example of how knowing new bike prices can help. Say you decide to want to buy a rugged urban commuting bike, made by Trek. At the time of writing, a new bike like this could cost you anywhere from $529.99 for a Trek Earl, to $2,649.99 for a Trek Valencia. That's a wide range of costs, and a wide range of quality. The equivalent used bikes reflect an even wider range of costs. A quick check on Craigslist turned up a used Trek Earl for $275, and two used Trek Valencias for $450. Of those two Valencias, one said it was a 2010, and the other said it was "a few years old." I would go for the one that was 2010, because the other could be much older, and because if the owner does not know the year, the bike could be stolen, or it could have had multiple owners. Also, if I could afford it I would go for the Valencia rather than the Earl, because the used price represents a greater savings on the new price of the Valencia, in comparison to the Earl. From this you can see that **it is worthwhile doing your research on new prices**.

One other thing to keep in mind is that big bike shops often have models that are from one to three years out of date. For example, they might be selling a 2010 bike in 2013. **You can often get an extremely good price on this old stock**, possibly even rivaling the price you would pay for the exact same bike in a used condition.

Research Used Bike Prices

Apart from new prices, you should also research current used prices. For example, **check what other sellers are asking for similar bikes on Craigslist, Kijiji, eBay, LesPAC, and other online market places**. Check the closing auction prices on eBay of similar bikes. This will give you a good idea of whether the seller's asking price is reasonable.

There are also some excellent **online cycling forums** where you can communicate with more experienced cyclists: ask them if the seller's asking price is fair, and see if anyone has experience of the particular bike you have in mind. You can get a lot of useful information, for free. In return, you will soon be able to give advice yourself!

Bear in mind that the **year of manufacture** makes a huge difference. For example, some of the newer Raleighs are very good, but many of the older ones are real clunkers. The rule of thumb for assessing the quality of new Raleighs is much like with all new bikes – you tend to get what you pay for.

On the other hand, it is much harder to know the value of older bikes. For example, the Raleigh Royale below

is very old, but it's actually a reasonably decent bike, and someone spent a lot of effort on restoring it (after paying just one dollar for it online!). The finished bike is shown below – the new owner turned it into a fixie (see http://www.fixedgear.co.nz/conversion.shtml). While the price he paid for the old bike was excellent, it took him 12 hours of skilled labor to convert it. Which is a lot if you can do it yourself, and too much if you have to pay someone else.

Also, a bike that is only a year old is going to be a lot more expensive than one that is ten years old. However, once a bike is more than about 30 years old it might qualify as a vintage bike, and then it could be as expensive as current models, and possibly even more expensive.

Of course, you have to do your research and make sure that a bike really is a **quality vintage bike**. Moreover, you should have a good reason for buying a vintage bike. Generally if you only have one bike and you want to use it for casual recreational use, you should not be looking at vintage bikes. These could turn out to be higher maintenance than you want or need.

If you do want a vintage bike, **don't be fooled just because the advert says "Rare" or "Vintage."** Don't take the seller's word for it – check for yourself!

Check the Condition of the Bike Before you Buy

Once you've done all your research, it's time to get out there and look at some of the advertised bikes. When you do this, you should check as much as you possibly can. Of course, this will depend a lot on your level of bike knowledge, but do your best to check at least the following:

- ☐ **Bottom bracket –** hold both cranks and try to move them from side to side. This should not be possible (indicates a loose bottom bracket).
- ☐ **Brakes –** do they work? If they don't, are they rusted solid or do they just have loose/broken cables? The brake cables and the plastic sheath around them should be rust-free and should not be frayed. If they are, they will need to be replaced.
- ☐ **Cables –** check for rusted, kinked or broken cables.
- ☐ **Chain –** condition – check the condition of the chain, as this will indicate how much use the bike has had. First of all, check if it's rusty, sagging or filthy. All of these are signs that the bike has had a lot of use or has not been well taken care of.

- ☐ **Chain –** wear and tear – even if the chain is clean and looks OK, it might still be almost worn out. Unfortunately it's hard (actually pretty much impossible) to check how much wear the chain has had with the naked eye. Which means people can pass off a bike that has had a lot of use as "barely used," and get away with it. So if you're serious about getting a good bike deal, you might want to invest in a little tool called a chain wear indicator (pictured on the previous page). It costs less than $20, and allows even technical novices to immediately assess how much wear the chain has had. You simply rest the tool on the chain and see how far down it sinks. If it's saying the chain has 75% wear and the seller says the bike is "barely used," you know the seller is lying (because the chain cannot go out all on its own, it has to take the rest of the bike with it!) This can alert you to not trust anything else the seller says.
- ☐ **Forks –** look at them carefully to check they are parallel. Make sure the forks cannot move forwards and backwards in the frame (which would indicate the headset is loose).
- ☐ **Frame –** should not be damaged or bent in any way. Run your hands along it to check for dents

or cracks. Look from the side at the areas where the top and down tubes meet the head tube. If you see a dent or a bulge in these areas, the bike has probably been in a crash that has damaged the frame. Do not buy a bike with a damaged frame!

- ☐ **Pedals –** while pedals are not very expensive, significant wear and tear on pedals indicates they have been around the block a few times – as in millions of times.
- ☐ **Rust –** check steel frames carefully for excessive rust, as it's impossible to get rid of, and it indicates the owner has not loved and cared for the bike. A little surface rust is acceptable, but serious rust can weaken the bike and make it dangerous.

- ☐ **Seat post –** can you move it? Sometimes these have rusted solid, meaning you will not be able to adjust the seat to your optimal height. These can be extremely hard to get unstuck, so if the saddle is at the wrong height and you cannot move it, you should probably pass.
- ☐ **Spokes –** check for loose, damaged, missing or bent spokes, which cause a lot of problems.
- ☐ **Tires –** if the tires are really worn, the bike has seen a lot of use, and a decent set of tires will cost you quite a bit of money. Also, the tires should not be dried or cracked.

☐ **Wheels** – first of all, they obviously should not be badly bent (like the one in the photo on the right, from http://forums.skateperception.com/). However, some wheel damage is less obvious. So you need to check if the wheels are true (i.e., not wobbly). Pick up each end of the bike and spin the wheel, looking out for a wobble. If you keep your eye on a fixed point, such as a brake pad, you will be able to see if parts of the wheel pass by it more closely than others. A slight wobble might indicate the rim has to be replaced. If there is a significant wobble the wheel is useless, and the bike might have had a pretty serious accident, which might have damaged something else as well.

As you can see, there are quite a lot of things to check. So if there is a bike you are serious about looking at, and you don't know anything at all about bikes, try to take along a friend who does.

If you don't have a knowledgeable friend, your best bet is to get a bike shop to assess the condition of the bike for you. To achieve this, it's helpful to have a good relationship with a bike shop. If you don't because this is your first bike, you could always let them know that you will be bringing all your future business to them once you find a bike. A good bike shop will usually oblige, even if it's just to give you a quick "Run away!" or "Looks pretty good."

Ride before you Buy

It's absolutely essential to get on the bike and ride it before you buy it. This applies even if you are buying a new bike. Fit and comfort will dictate whether you will actually use the bike, after all. And it's really hard to predict. You may know your size, but a particular brand in that size may not suit your body. So check all of the following points:

- ☐ Do you feel too stretched out?
- ☐ Can you see where you are going without hurting your neck?
- ☐ Do your back or shoulders hurt?
- ☐ Could you comfortably stay in this position for an hour or more?
- ☐ Can your hands comfortably reach and control the brakes and gears? (This can be a problem for those with smaller hands, which is why many bike manufacturers now make women-specific bikes.)

Also, if you ride a used bike up and down the street a few times, you will quickly discover whether the gears and brakes are working correctly. (Check that at least one of the brakes is working before you even start riding!) Watch out for gears that stick or jump. These problems may be easily fixed, but they may also be expensive fixes if the damage is great.

So before you buy a bike, adjust the seat height to suit you, put on a helmet, check the brakes are working, and take it for a spin down the nearest road. Be sure to change the gears all the way up and down while you are riding!

Red Flags to Watch out For

There are some excellent bargains to be found online, for those who have patience and some knowledge. However, some of the advertised bikes are rusting relics that someone wants to offload. Others are so hot they're sizzling (that is, just stolen).

While stolen bikes may be cheap, buying them is supporting the horrible people who bring great unhappiness to their victims when they steal their often-beloved bikes. Besides, in most jurisdictions if you are found with a stolen bike you are in the wrong, whether you knew it was stolen or not. You will have to give the bike to the police, you will almost certainly not be able to get your money back from the thief you bought it from, and you may face legal prosecution. So you really don't want to go there!

Fortunately, **there are many red flags to help you figure out which bikes should be avoided.** Here are some of the most important ones.

- ☐ The same bikes keep getting **reposted** over and over and over again. If they were such a bargain, wouldn't someone buy them?
- ☐ And when those unwanted bikes are reposted every single day, it's also a serious red flag. If someone is this desperate, this could be his or her main form of income, and therefore the person might be a bike thief. BUT do bear in mind that some people take pride in fixing and selling old bikes, and some even do it as a social service. So some of these adverts could be from genuine people who have lovingly restored a good bike. If that's the case, you couldn't buy from a better person, generally speaking. **If in doubt, talk to the seller on the phone**. It won't take you long to get a pretty good sense of who you are dealing with. For example, I once called someone who wanted to meet me at a transit station,

Red Flags

immediately, and who would knock $50 off the $200 price tag if I could get there in 30 minutes. The man sounded edgy and slightly manic. I got a very strong impression I was talking to a bike thief who was feeding a drug habit. So even though the bike was a great bargain, I passed it up.

- Always ask a couple of questions about the history of the bike, such as "How old is it?" and "Did you buy it new?" and "How much have you used it?" **If someone becomes cagy or defensive** when asked questions about the history of the bike, run away. If however the seller is happy to talk openly about the history of the bike, you are probably talking to an ethical seller. I know that one of my best buys was from a lovely woman who candidly shared that she had almost never ridden her bike because of back surgery, and showed me where the bike had been stored in her garage for three years. Before I left, she rummaged around and found several brand new accessories still in their boxes, including an expensive front light! I had a great feeling about that bike, and it turned out to be a great buy. It was a 2007 Trek 7.5 FX – three years old, yet essentially brand new. It's now an essential part of our bike tours.

☐ Watch our for lots of superlatives, such as these, from an actual ad:

**"incredible bike – I love this bike so much, it is a total head turner and people are always asking me where they can find one! ...
... black beauty ... work of art ... sexy bike!"**

The worst thing about this ad was that it did not mention the brand, model, size or age of the bike – although it included a photo of what looked like a department store bike with low-end parts! Basically, strings of superlatives may be used when there are no solid facts that would sell the bike.

☐ If the seller **posts a generic photo of the bike**, it could be a red flag. It could mean he or she does not want to post a photo of the real bike, because the real bike has recently been stolen from someone who might be scanning the online ads, watching out for it. This is not always true – some people just haven't mastered digital photography. But do take it as a warning sign. In general, it is far better to see a photo such as the one below, which is clearly someone's personal photo, not a generic photo off a bike web site.

Phrases to Watch out For, and What they REALLY Mean

- "I don't really know anything about bikes." Watch out for this; because it might mean: "I know the bike is wrecked/bent/broken beyond hope, so I want to pretend ignorance so that you won't phone back and yell at me when it falls apart." Of course, it might also just mean they don't know anything about bikes – which is all right if **you** do.
- "My roommate left it behind." This could mean all kinds of things, such as "I know the bike is wrecked/bent/broken beyond hope, so I want to pretend ignorance so that you don't phone back and yell at me when it falls apart," or **"It's stolen"**.

- "The photo doesn't show a saddle but I do have one/you can buy one really cheap." Most likely this means **"It's stolen"**. (Because some people remove their saddles when they park their bikes, to discourage bike thieves, but sadly it doesn't always work.)
- "The photo doesn't show a front wheel but I do have one/you can buy one really cheap." – **"It's stolen"**. (Because some people take off their front wheels when they park their bikes, to discourage bike thieves, but again, this doesn't always work.)
- "Must sell this bike today!" – **"It's stolen"**.
- If someone is selling a bike and says "Barely used!" or "Ridden only 4 times!" – well, there may be a very good reason why it's barely been used. And

Watch Out!

Average Joe Cyclist Guide

the reason may be that it's a horrible bike and a horrible ride. And if the current owner hates it that much, why would you want to pay money to ALSO have a bike that you don't want ride? (BUT if they have a really good reason for not riding it – such as back surgery – that's a whole different story. And let's not forget that many people buy bikes with good intentions of taking up cycling and getting fit, but then don't follow through. Of course, that will **not** happen to you!)

☐ "Rare!" "Vintage!" "Seldom found!" – Usually these phrases mean there is nothing good to say about the bike, so the seller hopes you will believe that it is a rare gem that you should buy before anyone else notices it ... and usually, the bike is not at all rare, as you will quickly discover if you do a bit more searching on the Internet.

Moronic Sellers to Watch out For!

Then there are the moronic posters. And boy, are there a lot of them! Watch out for these ones, because it really is better to buy a used bike from someone who knows what they are talking about. Therefore, generally try to avoid the following:

- ☐ **People who post and repost and repost** – apparently believing that if they keep advertising the same worthless bike at the same outrageous price for long enough, they will eventually find someone even more stupid than them, who will buy it. Some of them even put the price up when it doesn't sell for months! (However, there are sometimes valid reasons for re-posting – see "Making Lemonade" on p. 56.)
- ☐ **Sellers who think that "old" is spelled "vintage"** – When will these sellers realize that we know that a worthless bike that is really old is still worthless? Just because it is old, it does not miraculously morph into a "vintage" bike that is worth hundreds of dollars. In almost every advert I have ever seen that had the word "vintage," the word merely meant "old." Of course, writing off

all bikes labeled "vintage" would be a problem if you are actually looking for a real vintage bike (and there are sometimes some of these for sale online). Again, it's a case of doing your research to verify the seller's claim.

☐ **People who over price their bikes** – There are a lot of these, but provided you have done your research and know what new bikes cost, you will probably spot these right away. Another clue is that over-priced bikes will usually be posted over and over and over again. Bear in mind that when you buy a used bike, you don't get a warranty, or any after-sales service or care. Not to mention that the used bike may have been thrashed for years. So a used bike better be a lot cheaper than the equivalent new bike, to make it worthwhile! Do whatever you can to reassure yourself that it is a good price, including checking new prices, and doing a Google search for similar products online.

☐ **People who say "the bike comes with Shimano gears"** – OK, this does not mean that there is anything actually wrong with the bike. It's just an annoyingly stupid thing to say. Given that Shimano has pretty much cornered the entire market on bike gears, this is like saying "the car comes with four wheels!" And given that Shimano gears range from very poor quality to superlative quality, this tells the potential buyer precisely nothing about the bike. (If you know the type of Shimano gears, that's another story – see

"Kinds of Shimano Components" on p. 15.) Personally, the claim that a bike "has Shimano gears" always makes me wonder why the seller cannot find anything else to say about the bike. But again, this might just be stupidity, and does not necessarily mean there is anything wrong with the bike (bikes don't pick their owners, after all).

☐ **The countless advertisers who don't bother to mention the size of the bike –** How can you, the potential buyer, possibly know if the bike is any use to you, if you don't know its size? You might be 5 foot tall, and the bike being advertised would fit someone who is 6 foot tall! Bikes are not one-size-fits-all, and human beings come in all shapes and sizes. Again, this type of stupidity says more about the seller than the bike. However, it is certainly my pet peeve when it comes to moronic bike ads. Perhaps it's nothing but self-absorption taken to insane lengths: "Hey, it fits ME, so it'll fit anyone, because everyone is exactly my size!" And then there are the ads that say "man-sized" bike or "woman-sized" bike – um … now would that be my 5-foot-tall Uncle Pete, or my 6-foot-tall Aunt Emma? The problem with these ads is that they force potential buyers to waste time trying to find out the size. And once

you do make contact, you may find that the seller does not even know the size of the bike! This means the whole thing is just a waste of time, as I would not waste time and money driving across town to check out a bike if I did not even know its size.

- ☐ **Sellers who don't bother to mention the make or brand** – This just makes your life harder, as you cannot evaluate the bike if you just know that "it's a bike." In this case I just assume it's not a good brand, and ignore the ad.
- ☐ **Sellers who don't post a photograph, or post a generic photo** – It takes time and trouble to go and see a bike, so you should be able to see a photo first. Generic photos scare me as they might indicate a bike is stolen. Sometimes they are used so that the buyer cannot assess the age of the bike – see "Verify the Year of Manufacture" on p. 27.
- ☐ **Sellers who post almost no information on the bike** – Again, as it takes time and trouble to go and see a bike, you need a lot of information up front. As an example, someone recently advertised a Colnago on Craigslist. The text in the advert comprised just one word: "colnago"! Now admittedly, this one word speaks volumes in the cycling world, as Colnago is a great brand. Nonetheless, I found it very disrespectful to potential buyers to ask $750 for a used, old (vintage) bike, without having enough respect for prospective buyers to give any details or history of the bike. The seller hasn't given the buyer enough details to check whether this is a reasonable price.

Moronic Sellers

It might be a good buy, but the would-be seller should have taken the trouble to tell us about it. How many words would you type for $750? More than one, I'm guessing ... and I suspect you'd find the energy to hit the Shift key and achieve a capital letter. I know I would. I couldn't help thinking that if the seller did not have enough energy to type, he was unlikely to have had energy to maintain and clean this vintage bike for decades. This is one of those ads that tempts me to send a short email saying "Dude, are you kidding me?" – but unfortunately I'm far too nice to do that ... One thing's for sure though: I'm not giving $750 to someone who shows that little respect for prospective buyers.

- **Sellers who post nothing but generic cut-and-paste information –** It's fine to cut and paste the bike's specs and put them in an ad, as long as the seller also puts in some personal information, such as what condition the bike is in, how much it's been used, why it's being sold, etc. But just giving you the specs that the seller has obviously copied from another web site does not tell you anything you could not find on the internet yourself.

General Guidance from Bike Experts

There definitely are some great bargains to be found online, and I have found a couple myself ... so here is some general guidance to help you in your search for a bargain.

First of all, if the bike was originally bought at Sears or Walmart or Target or Canadian Tire or any other department store ... run away! (Admittedly there are some knowledgeable people who maintain that these places sometimes sell good bikes, but personally I have never seen one.) In general, department store bikes are heavier, weaker, and were originally assembled by someone who probably knew nothing about bikes. The components on these bikes will also be very low quality.

Beyond that, I reproduce here a piece of sage advice I found on the net from someone who calls himself "Retro Grouch". He starts by commenting on Apollo bikes, which pop up constantly in online ads, represented as "vintage" bikes:

"I have never seen an Apollo that was anything more than a utilitarian bike. And those were the better ones. I have seen hundreds – they are apparently a mandatory requirement of every yard sale, along with an unused exercise machine and Duran Duran cassette tapes. They typically are posted at a starting price of $20, but go unsold and end up in the landfill. Almost all Apollo's were bike boom junk that were ridden 100 km and then hung in the garage unused for the next 20 years. One of the recycling depots here in the lower mainland takes in and squashes dozens of these bikes per week."

Retro Grouch also offers sage advice for those who might be fooled by words such as "quality vintage bike made in Japan":

> "Here are the bikes that were nothing special at best, and before the mid-80s Yen shock, were dumped on our shores in the millions:
> - **Apollo**
> - **Kuwahara**
> - **Nishiki**
> - **Sekine**"

All of these bikes pop up regularly in online ads, usually described as "vintage" (which sounds so much better than "really, really old"). In fact, if you really want a laugh, go to an online market place and search for the word "vintage" under the Bikes for Sale …

On the other hand, experienced cyclist and blogger Raymond Parker (http://veloweb.ca/) has pointed out that Retro Grouch casts a wide net, and that Apollos and Sekines may be utilitarian, but many were well built and might still be trusty commuter bikes. Raymond has been riding his trusty Nishiki Landau for over 30 years. And highly respected cycling advocate Arno Schortinghuis

Guidance

(in the yellow jacket) says his Apollo has been his trusty commuter bike for many years. Just looking around while commuting on my bike, I notice that lots of people commute on Apollos. In fact, I have heard so much good about them that I have decided to get one myself and just see what it's like! However, I am not going to pay a premium price just because someone chooses to advertise it as a "rare Japanese bike"!

So it seems certain that all of the bikes listed by Retro Grouch should **not** simply be ignored – some may actually be decent bikes that you might be able to pick up at bargain prices. The key point here is going in with your eyes wide open (rather than being seduced by words like "vintage" or "rare find" or "much sought after"), doing your research – and finally, selecting a bike based on its quality and condition, providing you can get it at a fair price.

Good Quality Bikes made in the Last Couple of Decades

When it comes to bikes, **it is usually safe to judge quality based on brand and new price**. There are certain bike manufacturers who pretty much **only** make good quality bikes. When new, these are sold almost exclusively in bike shops – you will not find them in department stores such as Target, Canadian Tire, Sears or Walmart.

Each brand encompasses a range, ranging from lowest-level of quality frame and components, to highest-level of quality frame and components. The price range reflects the quality range. For example, an entry-level Devinci commuter bike would cost you $459 (the Devinci Milano, pictured below), while the top-of-the-range Devinci Sydney (on the right) would set you back more than three times as much – $1,599. Of course if you wanted a carbon-frame Devinci commuter, the Devinci Helsinki would set you back a cool $2,299. Ouch. Fortunately, the average cyclist really does not need a carbon-fibre bike.

Average Joe Cyclist Guide

So there is a wide range of quality and price. However, what you can be sure of is that **any bike made by one of these manufacturers was of reasonably good quality when it was manufactured and assembled**. Providing it has been reasonably well cared for and has not been used for purposes it was not designed for – such as a single-track mountain bike that has been used for downhill jumping – then it should still be a good quality bike.

You might wonder why you should bother to spend more money to get a quality bike. I know I used to wonder that, before I ever tried a good quality bike. I had an old Raleigh clunker, and I could hardly get up the tiniest of hills. I thought I was just horribly out of shape – until I tried a good quality bike. I was amazed at the difference it made, and since then I only ride good quality bikes. Good quality bikes give a better, more efficient ride.

Also, you are much safer on a good quality bike – it is not unheard of for department store bikes to literally fall apart on their first outing. They are, after all, assembled by people who may know nothing at all about bikes. Imagine a bike falling apart while you are on it – you could really do yourself a lot of damage.

So these are the better quality bike brands that are usually worth buying (in alphabetical order, not in order of preference):

Quality Bikes

Quality Bikes

- ☐ Argon
- ☐ Bianchi
- ☐ Brodie
- ☐ Brompton (for folding bikes)
- ☐ Cannondale (especially their road bikes)
- ☐ Cervelo
- ☐ Dahon (for folding bikes)
- ☐ Devinci (especially their hybrids)
- ☐ Diamond Back
- ☐ Eddie Merckx
- ☐ Felt
- ☐ Fuji
- ☐ Gary Fisher
- ☐ Ghost
- ☐ Giant
- ☐ GT
- ☐ Jamis
- ☐ KHS
- ☐ Kona (especially their mountain bikes)
- ☐ Kuota
- ☐ Le Mond (now part of Trek)
- ☐ Marin
- ☐ Norco (especially their mountain bikes)
- ☐ Pinarello
- ☐ Raleigh (not all of them, be discerning)

52   *Average Joe Cyclist Guide*

- ☐ Rocky Mountain
- ☐ Santa Cruz
- ☐ Schwinn (not all of them, be discerning – quality has been on the decline since these started being sold through big box stores)
- ☐ Scott
- ☐ Specialized (especially their road bikes)
- ☐ Surly
- ☐ Trek
- ☐ Univega

Note: if you're reading this and your favorite good-quality bike has been left out, please don't get mad – just **drop me a line via my blog (www.averagejoecyclist.com) and let me know.** I can always add your suggestion to the next edition of this guide. I have tried to list all the good-quality brand names, but I'm only human, so I may have missed one or two.

Good Quality Vintage Bikes

Buying older or genuine vintage bikes is much more tricky. Again it comes down to brand, but it's more difficult because things change over time. However, if you want to find a good vintage bike, here's advice from Retro Grouch:

"Here are the bikes to sell your soul for:
- Colnago
- Pinarello
- Cinelli
- Merckx
- Masi (the genuine older ones)
- Olmo (ditto)
- Pogliaghi
- De Rosa
- Litespeed"

To this list, I would also add Bridgestone. Unfortunately, I rarely see any of these for sale online.

The photo at the top of this page shows Albert Masi, son of Faliero Masi, an Italian master bike builder who built each custom bike with absolute care and thoroughness (photo from http://italiancyclingjournal.blogspot.ca/).

Average Joe Cyclist Guide

Bikes to Strenuously Avoid

Retro Grouch also warns about several bikes, and regrettably, these are all too common. He describes the bikes that must be strenuously avoided as follows:

"... these (bikes) are not good enough for a homeless bottle picker, even when new:
- **CCM**
- **Huffy**
- **Western Flyer**
- **Murray**
- **Infinity**
- **Motiv**
- **Free Spirit**
- **Supercycle**
- **Dunlop**
- **Pacific**
- **Mongoose**
- **Carerra**
- **Fila"**

Remember these names, and be wary of them! I have heard from some people that some of these bikes can be OK, so if the price is very low, the bike feels good to you, and this is the only bike you can afford right now, go for it. Any bike is better than no bike, and will provide a starting point to get into cycling. Just this morning I saw a woman riding a Supercycle to work – the bike was groaning and squeaking, but I admired the woman for getting it to move at all. Personally, I agree with Retro Grouch that these are bikes to be strenuously avoided, if you can afford better. If you can't, inspect them very carefully to try and make sure they don't fall apart while you're riding them.

Also, bear in mind that for the price many advertisers are asking for a used bike with one of the names above, you might be able to get a perfectly good bottom-of-the-range quality bike from your local bike shop. And most of those bikes come with lifetime guarantees on their frames.

Making Lemonade ... Dedicated Cyclists who Fix "Less Worthy" Bikes

Some cycling experts have pointed out to me that even a bike that seems to be worthless may turn out to be a solid enough bike for certain purposes, such as urban commuting. Raymond Parker's Veloweb blog features some of these in a really interesting post called Velos for Everyman (http://veloweb.ca/commuting/readers-commuter-bikes/). Bikes he features there include several that are routinely despised, including a fixed-gear, 30-year-old Sekine; the pictured six-year-old Iron Horse above, that does heavy commuting duty (the company went bust in 2009, and the bikes are usually considered sub-standard, but they have their fans); a five-year-old steel frame Redline 9.2.5.; and a $400 department store Raleigh. Most of these bikes have had some loving care and upgrades lavished on them by their adoring owners. Still, it goes to show that there is hope for almost any bike.

And then there's Blogger Ryan (http://thecitycyclist.blogspot.ca/), who takes pride in repairing cast-off bikes that some people look down upon, then selling them at a fair price on Craigslist or Kijiji. He repairs, cleans and test rides every bike he sells. He says he sees his work as:

"doing a double service. Keeps a bike out of the landfill and gives new life to something that would otherwise be deemed no good."

Ryan even repairs department store bikes, and he points out that he has to re-post his ads because new people are always looking, and because so many people post on these popular sites that one's advert quickly gets pushed out of sight.

So the point is, there are some very decent, knowledgeable people providing good bikes online, at very good prices. You could be off and biking on a decent bike for under $100!

Photo from http://jonkiessel.com/

Should You Buy a "Sucky" Bike?

Of course, there is one big advantage to having a bike that is considered inferior: you can park it anywhere without having to worry about it. I actually bought just such a bike for $40 on Craigslist. It is rusted and old and ugly, but it goes pretty well, and I can park it anywhere. I use it when I have to do an errand in the rougher parts of town, where the danger of theft is higher. In fact, one humorous seller on Craigslist focused on this aspect in trying to sell his bike. He advertised it as a "sucky" bike, and highlighted all the reasons why no one would steal it. It must have worked, because he only posted it once!

Also, I know that some people choose to ride old clunkers because the extra weight helps them to get into shape faster, or increases their already high level of fitness. Personally, I need all the help I can get from the bike, so I would not deliberately pick a slow, heavy bike (hey, I'm kind of slow and heavy myself – I don't need my bike to be slow and heavy too!)

Bargains Can be Found!

As shown by the example of Ryan, there are some ethical people around who fix bikes and then sell them online. If you can find one of them, you may score an excellent bargain – and also keep a bike out of the landfill! Also, in affluent societies many people have valuable bikes that they simply don't use, and these often end up for sale at bargain prices.

For example, I own two great entry-level mountain bikes, a Norco and a Scott. I bought the Norco new, and the Scott on Craigslist. The Norco is an excellent bike, and cost me around a thousand dollars, with tax. The Scott is an excellent bike, and cost around $500 ($450 to the seller, and $50 to the bike shop to get it perfect). The bikes have near identical components. The Norco rides slightly better than the Scott, but it is not $500 better, and it is definitely **not twice as good**. For the purposes I use mountain bikes, **both** bikes are perfectly adequate. Have a look at the photos – do you think one of these bikes is worth double what the other

one is? Of course, the Scott did not come with a warranty, but I have never needed a warranty on either of them as they are both in perfect condition.

In short, it is possible to meet one's cycling needs for around half the cost by buying a used bike – and sometimes even for less. And after all, even a new bike becomes used after you've used it for a day …

In fact, I have to say that I got my best bike deal ever on Craigslist (and that one great deal is probably why I am still hopelessly addicted). It's this 1990 Bridgestone MB-2, loving and cleverly crafted in the days when basic mountain bikes were made amazingly well. These were made in Japan, under the direction of master bike designer Grant Petersen, and mine is a pure joy to ride. In fact it is more fun to ride than any of my other bikes, but I bought it on Craigslist for a couple of hundred dollars. It had not been very well cared for, but it also had not been ridden much or trashed, so it needed minimal work to be back in fine running form. Love this bike! Of course, I only knew that this was a great buy because I had done a lot of research about Bridgestone bikes – all on the Internet.

So there are great bikes to be found on Craigslist, Kijiji or other sites, but you have to ride a lot of frogs first …

Tips for Selling Bikes Online

When the time comes to sell your bike, make life easier for yourself and potential buyers by following these guidelines:
1. Mention the **make** of bike (such as Trek, Specialized, Raleigh, Fuji, Mongoose, etc.).
2. Also mention the **model** of bike in as much detail as you possibly can (such as Trek Valencia, Specialized Secteur Triple, Raleigh Detour City Sport, Mongoose Crossway 150 Fem, etc.).
3. List the **year of manufacture** if you possibly can (such as 2011). If you don't know the year, give the age as accurately as you can (such as 2008). Don't try and fudge this one – bikes come out in specific colors in different years, so it is easy for a discerning buyer to know if you are lying about the age of the bike.
4. **Specify the size**. Please, please, please specify the size as accurately as you can (e.g. 15 inches for a mountain bike or hybrid, 54 cm for a road bike). If you don't know the specific size, at least try to figure out if it is a small, medium or large. It is also really useful to say something like "It fits me perfectly and I am 6'8"." That way people who are 5'2" don't have to waste their time coming to try out a bike they couldn't even climb onto. Failing to specify the size wastes your time, wastes the buyer's time, and is frankly, just plain stupid.
5. Include a recent, clear **photograph**. And it should be of the actual bike you are selling, not just some random bike that is similar. If you don't have a photo of the bike you are selling, it is harder for buyers to decide if they want it, and some people will assume the bike might be stolen.
6. Say (truthfully) **why you are selling** the bike, for example: "I have decided road bikes are not for me; selling this so I can buy a mountain bike."

7. Include some information on the **condition** of the bike, for example: "This bike is in as-new condition – I have used it about 30 times, mainly in dry weather, in urban conditions," or "This bike is in used but good condition – I have put several thousand miles on it, but I have maintained it well and it is still in great shape".
8. If you like, include details of **components and specs**. It is OK to copy this from a website.

Below is an example of a good advert for a used bike. Note that it has all the relevant information in the subject line, so buyers don't have to waste time clicking on the ad, only to find the bike is too small/too old/too expensive, etc.

For sale: 20 Trek 7.5 FX WSD (Women Specific Design), 15 inches. $300 obo. Would suit person around 5'3" with smaller hands. Selling this bike because I have had to quit cycling following knee surgery. The bike is lightly used – probably around 500 miles, in good weather conditions. Well maintained and recently serviced; ready to ride away. Includes rat-trap, mudflaps, lights. Great commuting bike! Asking $300.

A Closing Thought – Please be Nice to Bike Sellers

Ryan (http://thecitycyclist.blogspot.ca/), the guy who restores bikes and provides a great value for buyers, tells me that countless people arrange to come over and see a bike, then just don't show up – without so much as an email or a phone call to say they have changed their minds. Online market places offer the opportunity for people to satisfy their needs by buying or selling bikes. It can be a win-win situation. But to achieve this, we all have to be respectful of each other's time and money. Just as bike sellers shouldn't rip people off, bike buyers should respect the time of bike sellers.

Let's all just be decent and respectful of one another, and help make cycling fun for EVERYONE!

If you found this guide useful, you might also like:
**Average Joe Cyclist Guide:
How to Buy the Right Electric Bike**
(available on Kindle and Amazon)

and my cycling blog, **www.averagejoecyclist.com**, which has tons of free information

Ride On!

Read More!